SUNRISE TO SUNSET

Eight Devotions Inspired

by African Landscapes

DERYN VAN DER TANG

SUNRISE TO SUNSET
© 2020 Deryn van der Tang
All Rights Reserved.

Scripture quotations are taken from The Living Bible copyright © 1971. Used by permission of Tyndale House Publishers, a Division of Tyndale House Ministries, Carol Stream, Illinois 60188. All rights reserved.

ISBN-

Cover photograph ©2020 Deryn van der Tang
Sunrise to Sunset is written in American English.

Acknowledgements

I would like to thank Hannah Marie MacIntosh and Robert Read for their thoughtful suggestions, insight and editing.

A special thanks to Phillip Read for making the travel to Namibia and Victoria Falls possible and for the rest of the family for their encouragement along the way.

I would also like to thank Louise Morse and Justina Ford for their mentorship in my writing journey and CWOSA for their support and giving me this opportunity.

Table of Contents

Introduction

The places I have been and lived in Africa will always be a part of me. Hence my theme, "Landscapes." I was born in Rhodesia (Zimbabwe) and was entranced with the sunsets over the Zambezi River. The glory of African sunrises and sunsets cannot be beaten. I have memories of many a dawn call to go game viewing as well, but dawn in the Namibian desert was the most spiritual I have experienced. I wanted to share it with you, my readers.

The other themes of the sprightly springbok, climbing a mountain, the eagle and crossing the river, are all things that have been meaningful to me as I pursue my relationship with God, and I see how He can communicate with us through His creation. It was my joy to introduce my eldest son's new Finnish family to my land of birth.

1

Sunrise Over Namibia

"Very early on Sunday morning, just at sunrise, they went to the tomb."
(Mark 16:2)
"His coming is as brilliant as the sunrise. Rays of light flash from his hands, where his awesome power is hidden."
(Habakkuk 3:4)

It was our first trip to Namibia to show my new Finnish family Africa, the land of my birth. We had travelled to the Namib Naukluft Lodge as a base so we could see the desert. Our wakeup call was at 4:45am to have a mini breakfast before we set out for the Sossusvlei sand dunes.

The moon and stars were spectacular as we travelled in the dark. The magnificence of the night skies made us aware of how infinite the Universe is. The stars sparkled and twinkled in the thick velvet blackness, and the indigo silhouette of the distant mountains framed the bottom edge of this picture. The sickle moon and the morning star were set in place between the ridge of the mountains and the expanse of the skies above. It was a moment of timelessness, when we felt part of the picture and not detached from it.

Towards 6.00am, the first light of dawn started to show behind the ridge of mountains in the east, and the velvet blackness of the night sky slowly turned into pale blue. Fingers of sunlight faded the stars from sight. The sickle moon and morning star hung there a little longer before they took their closing bow when the curtain of daylight was finally lifted.

Moses and Aaron were the guardians of the Tabernacle in the wilderness and were told to camp on the east side towards the sunrise. Dawn is the time when your body, mind and soul are rested, and you can spend quiet time meditating, praying and worshiping God before other activities demand your attention. It is a time to wait on the Lord for instructions for the day ahead, to be thankful for new opportunities and a time to sit and be part of the greater picture of things. Your individual importance disappears as it is absorbed into the ebb and flow of the common experience of those around us.

The soft blush of daybreak brightens as the sun rises higher in the sky; the shadows are softer at first light. I like to think that dawn is the space for new beginnings, new thoughts, new attitudes, new deeds, a time for new perspectives before they become hardened dogmas and points of view. Sunrise gives me space to think of the greater good, that I am merely one mortal among thousands. We all take our place in the overall welfare of mankind by the actions that come from our waking up and starting each day right. Let the softness of love be our shadows and not the sharp edges drawn by the noonday sun.

It was dawn when Mary found the empty tomb. Jesus, also called the *bright and morning star,* conquered the final enemy, death. Seeing the morning star shine so brightly in the desert reminded me of the importance of dawn and our starting the day right.

▪How important is it that we honor the first few hours of each new day in spiritual practice?

▪In what way can you see this make a difference to your day?

▪What part can you play today in the greater good?

 *Dear God, thank you that I can wake up to a new day. Your mercies are sufficient to cover what this day has in store for me.*

2

Your Destiny is in the Desert

"He changes rivers into deserts, and springs of water into dry,
thirsty land."
(Psalm 107:35)
"Restore our fortunes, Lord, as streams renew the desert."
(Isaiah 35:1)

The rocky outcrops gradually turned into sand dunes and the vegetation became very sparse in the arid conditions of the Namib Desert. We saw ostrich and springbok as they searched for food amongst rock and dry scrub along the way. We drove to the entrance of the Sossusvlei National Park, where we transferred into 4 x 4 vehicles equipped for driving in the dry sandy riverbed which served as a road. The vehicle slithered and bucked along this track until we arrived at the Kameeldoring picnic spot. Here the driver unpacked a picnic breakfast which was most welcome. A flock of sparrows jostled and tweeted waiting for crumbs. They obviously knew the breakfast drill! One brave sparrow jumped onto my shoe and tried to snatch food from my hand.

The undulating dunes were on every side of us with their high, sharp curved ridges and hollowed wind-carved sides. The great purple shadows and patterns thrown by the sunlight make these dunes a photographer's paradise. We set off to climb Dune 17, Big Mamma. We walked along the ridge. It was not too difficult walking, but progress was slow. Near the top I decided to stop and just "be" so I could have a time of quiet. Walking with the group was a distraction from my desert experience.

To me, a desert experience needed to be a time of total silence and solitude when I could just listen to God's voice with no distraction. I sat with my fingers sifting through the sand of the dune. I listened to the silence; it was palpable. Not a sound, not a cry of a bird or even the sound of voices as the tour group disappeared over the ridge. It was a moment of being at one with the sand, one with the space around me, isolated in the middle of the vast acres of sand, yet quite at peace as I let the silence fill me. I watched an ant run down the side of the dune and a desert lizard make its way across the sand.

I wondered how creatures could live in such a harsh environment. Although the desert appeared to be dead, it was still very much alive. The longer I sat there the more I realized I was not alone!

I thought of Moses and the burning bush, Jesus' temptation in the wilderness, and all those desert fathers who went into the wilderness to find 'something'. There is a saying 'your destiny is determined in the desert.' It is during those times of dryness and apparent lifelessness that thoughts and temptations to give up make their presence felt. It is during the dry times in our life, the times when we do not have the energy or the inclination to move forward, when we feel empty, that we thirst for something bigger than ourselves to take over.

Once you have experienced the overwhelming desolation of the desert, you will never be the same. When the deep place of silence filters into the very core of your being, that is where you meet with God and return, ready to continue with your mission in life. There is a paradox in this experience; before we can flow with renewed energy, we need this time of dryness to push our roots deeper into God.

As I sat there on the ridge, the silence became a song, I could just feel the praise and worship welling up like a spring of inner joy. Prayer flowed naturally as a conversation with God. I prayed for rain as it was so dry, and I prayed for hope for the future. When I felt full and complete after being in this holy place, I set off down the dune again to join the rest of the group at the vehicle and we drove back to the Namib Naukluft Lodge. This desert experience was one I will never forget, enabling me to experience a heightened encounter of God's presence.

▪When do you feel the need for solitude and renewal?

▪After a period of dryness in your life, did you bloom again with renewed vision and energy?

 *Thank you God for the times of dryness when our soul thirsts for something bigger than ourselves. You refresh us from within, with your Living Water.*

3

As Surefooted as the Springbok

"As the deer longs for streams of water, so I long for you, O God.
I thirst for God, the living God. When can I go and stand before him?"
(Psalm 42:1-2)
"Her princes are like starving deer searching for pasture. They are too
weak to run from the pursuing enemy"
(Lamentations 1:6)

During our drive through Namibia, we were privileged to see several groups of springbok grazing in the arid veld as they searched for the odd blade of grass or root. These fascinating deer with their characteristic white faces, black stripes, tan triangle on their forehead, and curved horns are probably South Africa's most iconic animal. When alarmed, they have an unusual way of jumping. They 'pronk' extremely high with stiff legs while they run, which is quite unique to them. Living in the dry and arid regions of Southern Africa, they have adapted well to their rocky surroundings, feeding off scrub and some grasses. They have a preference for plants that have a higher water content such as roots or flowers when in season. Their large herds migrate across great distances searching for food and water.

For me, the springbok represents one of the Biblical metaphors of surefootedness and thirsting after God. These beautiful creatures make an amazing sight when they 'pronk'. They can jump vertically up to three-and-a-half meters high and then land perfectly on all four hooves before 'pronking' off again. The Old Testament mentions on numerous occasions that "He makes me as surefooted as a deer, enabling me to stand on mountain heights." Deer are God's messengers of stability when we are navigating difficult territory. When we are alarmed, afraid, or running from danger, we can head for the higher ground knowing that we will still be able to stand. We will overcome, even though fighting the enemy is on difficult terrain. The Lord will guide our footsteps and we can stand securely in the knowledge that His presence is with us at all times.

Yet there are times when we just cannot seem to connect with God. We yearn for His comfort and presence. It is in those times of spiritual drought that, like the springbok, we travel through the desolate places searching for refreshment. Our hearts long for God and we lament that we are like starving deer searching for pasture, too weak to fight off the enemy. There are times we feel too vulnerable to carry on when God is nowhere to be found. We feel we are about to fall into the hands of the enemy because our resistance has weakened. We long for God to rescue us. The springbok knows a predator will catch them in their weakened state if they do not continue to search for the stream or waterhole or dig until they find a root to give them sustenance. Sometimes we too have to dig a very deep well to find that spring of water in the desert, or spend time searching the Scriptures for that root that will take us to the promise of God's help and presence in times of need.

•Where do you run to when you are afraid?

•Are you satisfied with the small 'nibbles' or are you looking for the flowing stream or waterhole?

God, sometimes it is hard to find you when we search for you and long for you to rescue us from our enemies. Lead us to the water, sustain us with your words, let us find our stability in your Presence.

4

Reaching the Summit

"A song for pilgrims ascending to Jerusalem. I look up to the mountains— does my help come from there?"

(Isaiah 49:13)

"I press on towards the goal to win the prize for which God has called me heavenwards in Christ Jesus. All of us who are mature should take such a view of things. And if on some point you think differently that too God will make clear to you. Only let us live up to what we have already attained".

(Phil 3:14-16)

I had been living in Cape Town for several years and enjoyed the beautiful walks and hikes around Table Mountain. One of my goals was to see the wildflowers in the Overberg, but for various reasons I had not been able join a hiking group to do it. I planned a weekend away with my other son to visit the area and do the ten-kilometer hike through the Caledon Wildflower Garden and environs. We stayed at the Caledon Hotel, so we could enjoy the hot spring water in the Victorian Bath House as well.

We were well prepared with adequate clothing, shoes and refreshments, and we set off with a map to guide us. We anticipated a pleasant and leisurely walk through the beautiful countryside at wildflower time. We found the trail and started to walk; enjoying the scenery, the fresh air, and the fact we were at last on our way to fulfill my dream.

We stopped occasionally to enjoy the flowers and the view. Winding its way out of the gardens at the far end, the path became narrower and a bit steeper and it took more effort to walk. We slowed our pace a bit, but I got tired. My legs ached, and blood pounded through my temples as the pathway wound its way upwards. We met unexpected difficulties crossing a vlei and small stream and our shoes got wet. We had to stop frequently for me to take a breather and a sip of water.

The path continued to wind steeply upwards, unrelenting as we headed for the top of the mountain (which was not shown on the map!). We persevered. My goal was to complete this hike. My son patiently waited for me so I could rest often, and encouraged me along the way. As we approached the summit, the way became very rough and stony. The pathway almost disappeared. In places, I had to crawl on all fours to make my way upward. How I wished there was an easier way, but I had to persevere. There was no turning back. We were closer to the top than the gardens at the bottom. To go back would have been just as difficult as well as an admission of defeat of my dream. I chose to keep moving forward with every step, no matter how difficult it was and however tired I felt.

Eventually, we reached the summit and saw the world stretched out below us. It was breathtaking in every direction, despite the freezing wind. We had a whole new perspective and could see the path we had travelled in the distance, far below. We pointed to obstacles we had overcome. They looked so small from up there. We sheltered behind a rock and rested awhile before it was time to climb back down. The descent was just as difficult. The path was unclear. The way was strewn with boulders, stones, and loose gravel. We slipped and stumbled our way down. We did not require as much rest although it was just as difficult, but eventually we arrived back at the car having attained our goal and fulfilled my dream.

After this experience, I reflected on my Christian walk. I wondered, do I expect everything to be easy without obstacles and difficulties, traversing life's pathways? No. Difficulties will always be there, trials of our faith and character are part of our growth to become more Christlike. Just as my son was there to encourage me, Jesus has promised to be with us and never leave nor forsake us. When we have started out and difficulties arise, do we doubt we are on the right road? Not if we are sure we're going the way the Lord has directed us. The goal is still there. The way may not be clear, but the goal does not change. Our human frailty does get in the way and we may have to stop to take a breath to be refreshed but we do not give up. Lack of resources may slow the process down, but that does not change our goal or mission.

I once saw an old priest on his bicycle in the middle of the tsetse-fly-ridden Zambezi Valley in Zimbabwe. He was hundreds of kilometers from anywhere, going to serve his people. How many of us would be prepared to go to that length to serve?

We can become enthusiastic with the vision and set a good goal for ourselves. This is the exciting part, the beginning of the journey, just as I had eagerly planned the trip to Caledon to visit the Wildflower Gardens. Once we are physically involved in reaching that goal, difficulties and problems become apparent. We may feel like giving up. Self-doubt sets in and we wonder if we are really on the right path. Did we fully understand our calling? Or have we perhaps taken a wrong turn somewhere and we are headed in the wrong direction? Our enthusiasm wanes, we are discouraged and the motivation to attain the goal diminishes.

We need to persevere and not grow weary but know that the Lord is with us. Our map is His Word which is a guide and a lamp for our feet. He knows the obstacles we face. They are there as learning tools. We are encouraged by His Word and our fellow travelers along the way, and we can rest in Him from time to time.

Yes, the upward slog is hard, but when you reach the summit or attain your goal, the hard work will be worth it. You will see what has been accomplished from a higher perspective. Keep going!

•In what times in your life do you feel it is just too hard to keep going?

•Who can you ask, or what can you do, for some encouragement to continue the journey?

 *Lord, we look to you when the going gets tough, sometimes we think we are just not going to make it.*

Help us to persevere. Your Presence is always there to encourage us and your Word there to guide us.

5

Soaring Like an Eagle

"Even youths will become weak and tired, and young men will fall in exhaustion. But those who trust in the Lord will find new strength. They will soar high on wings like eagles. They will run and not grow weary. They will walk and not faint."

(Isaiah 40:30-31)

"He fills my life with good things. My youth is renewed like the eagle's! The Lord gives righteousness and justice to all who are treated unfairly."

(Psalm 106:5,6)

As we stood at the top of the Overberg mountain and looked as far as the eye could see, my son pointed out two eagles as they circled high on the thermals. We were amazed to think that the eagles could see prey far below, where we could only make out the larger objects. Small things merged into a colored blur. Eagles can have a wingspan of up to two meters across, they soar to great heights and look graceful and effortless as they let the thermal currents carry them. They have clear vision and patience to wait for the appropriate moment to strike, then, from a great height they swoop down in seconds onto their prey.

The eagle has significant symbolism in mythology, human culture, and in Christianity. As an artist, I love the spiritual metaphors of the Bible. What is it about the eagle that lends itself to the mystery and symbolism of God's Word?

Initially, God spoke through nature and through creation, so that man would have no excuse for not seeing Him as the Creator God. In the Church of England, it is tradition to place the Bible on the outstretched wings of a bronze eagle.

When an eagle catches a snake, it does not fight it on the ground. It picks it up and flies up with it, then drops it back to the ground. A snake has no stamina, power or balance in the air. It is useless, weak and vulnerable, whereas on the ground it is deadly, wise and powerful. The eagle teaches us to take our battles to the spiritual realm as it lifts its lethal and toxic prey away from where it can do damage. When you take problems that can harm you to the spiritual realm and pray for deliverance from evil, God takes charge. Don't fight these battles in the physical realm—move to a higher realm, like an eagle. You will be assured of a clear victory.

I see this symbol as the power of the Holy Spirit rising above the earth, a freedom rising above the material to see spiritual things, power, balance, dignity and grace, attaining a higher truth, the messenger between heaven and earth. We should be waiting for that moment of Divine truth when the Holy Spirit is ready to use us and work through us.

The metaphor of the eagle teaches us that we can trust in the Lord with patient expectation. He will fulfill the promises in His Word to strengthen us to rise above life's difficulties. He will protect us from evil. God loves us and wants the best for us, so we can relax and be confident that His purposes are right. We need to be fully convinced that He has the power to control all of life as well as ours. Though our faith may be weak or struggling, we can accept His provision, protection, and care for us.

We are encouraged by Isaiah's words that even young people will get tired and give up. But if we wait on the Lord, He will give us renewed energy and strength for the battle. The Psalmist also used the eagle as a symbol of renewed energy as he was praising God for His help against injustice.

Sometimes we may feel insignificant and helpless as we struggle against unjust systems. When we get weary it is good to remember the battle is not ours. The war is against the principalities and powers of darkness. When we take our issues up into the spiritual realm, our Lord will fight them with His heavenly army.

After our refreshing break at the top of the Overberg mountain, my son and I took one last look at the eagles as they effortlessly soared and circled above us. We made our way down the mountain back into the physical realm of practical daily living. We had learnt a valuable spiritual lesson from the eagles. Anxiety ends where faith begins, when we take our battles off the ground to a higher plane.

▪What Battles are you facing that need to be taken off the physical to the spiritual realm?

▪Do you believe that God's justice will prevail in the end?

Father, sometimes I feel so weary of life's battles. I see injustice and unfairness all around me. It impacts my life, my family and community's life. There seems no ending to the struggles. Please may I just hand them to you?

6

Crossing the River

"When you go through deep waters, I will be with you. When you go through rivers of difficulty, you will not drown. When you walk through the fire of oppression, you will not be burned up; the flames will not consume you."

(Isaiah 43:2)

"And I will fix your boundaries from the Red Sea to the Mediterranean Sea, and from the eastern wilderness to the Euphrates River."

(Exodus 23:31)

"But you will soon cross the Jordan River and live in the land the Lord your God is giving you. When he gives you rest from all your enemies and you're living safely in the land, you must bring everything I command you."

(Deuteronomy 12:10)

No visit to showcase Africa to our Finnish family would have been complete without a visit to one of my favorite places, the Victoria Falls and the mighty Zambezi River. When you walk through the forest when the river is full, you get soaked to the skin with spray whether you wear rain clothes or not. The local name for the Falls is 'Mosi-oa-Tunya, "The Smoke that Thunders," because the noise of the water is so loud you cannot hear yourself speak. David Livingstone was the first European to discover these falls. His statue stands near to the Devil's Cataract where a rainbow forms over the falling water.

The Victoria Falls is a great tourist attraction and World Heritage site, where a lot of adventure sports like white water rafting and bungee jumping can be experienced. The Zambezi River serves as the northern boundary between Zimbabwe and Zambia. The far northwestern tip of Zimbabwe is where the Caprivi Strip, Botswana, and Zambia all meet at the Zambezi river which serves as boundary to all four states.

This ancient river starts in the upper reaches of Zambia near the Congo border. After the Victoria Falls, it flows through Lake Kariba and the Cahora Bassa Hydro Electric scheme which provides electricity and water management for the region. It finally makes its way through Mozambique into the Indian Ocean.

We took a helicopter trip above the waterfall and along the river. The sinuous ribbon of water lay far below us, dotted with islands. We saw it rush its way to the gorge where it fell in thundering chaos over the precipice to the bottom of the ancient chasm carved out over eons and then on to its destination.

The southern border of Zimbabwe is demarcated by the 'great, grey, greasy Limpopo River' as Rudyard Kipling described it. Rivers form natural boundaries for countries and wars have been fought to hold their ground, often being the place where the battle was lost or won.

God said he would fix the boundaries of the Promised Land from the Red Sea to the Mediterranean Sea, and from the eastern wilderness to the Euphrates River. Crossing the Jordan has become a metaphor for transitions. When the Israelites entered the Promised Land, the Jordan parted. They went across to start a new life in the land of milk and honey.

The River Jordan again parted when Elijah crossed and ascended to heaven after giving his mantle to Elisha, transitioning him into his new prophetic role. Another personal transition took place when Naaman dipped in the river and his leprosy was healed. After wrestling with God at the River Jabbok, Jacob was named Israel, as he transitioned to become the father of the Israelites.

Crossing the Jordan can also be a metaphor for transitioning from spiritual darkness into spiritual awakening. John the Baptist baptized Jesus in the River Jordan, transitioning the New Covenant when the heavens opened to announce that this was God's Son and from this time our centuries would now be counted from AD instead of BC.

When I crossed the Limpopo River into South Africa, I left one country and culture and transitioned into another. There was also the national transition in November 1965 when our country, which was known as Rhodesia, changed from being a self-governing British territory to an independent sovereign state which would eventually be known as Zimbabwe.

There are also personal transitions, from being married to being widowed. One day, we will all face our final 'crossing the Jordan,' a euphemistic term for death. Christ's atoning death on the cross and resurrection assures us that those who believe in Him, when we exit this life, will transition into our new heavenly life. "Crossing the river" is a timeless metaphor for death in mythology and different cultures where various rituals are practiced to help the person into the afterlife.

As we completed our visit to the Victoria Falls and the Zambezi, I realized how difficult transitions can be. We had to adjust to our new state of being part of the Finnish family, just as they had to adjust to being part of our African family. We can be encouraged by the Word of God. Jesus says He will be with us as we go through these difficult times and adapt to our new circumstances. We also learn to set boundaries that keep us safe and preserve our authentic selves so that the transition does not change who we are, but enriches us.

•What transitions have you made where you had to metaphorically 'cross the river'?

•What are your thoughts and fears around the final 'crossing the Jordon?'

•What boundaries do you need to set?

Father God, there are times that I am overwhelmed, and I need to hold my ground and set boundaries. There are times when you have set my boundaries and I must trust that you will be with me and I will not be overcome.

7

Sunset Over the Zambezi

"And don't sin by letting anger control you. Don't let the sun go down while you are still angry."

(Ephesians 4:26)

"There was a man named Nicodemus, a Jewish religious leader who was a Pharisee. After dark one evening, he came to speak with Jesus. "Rabbi," he said, "we all know that God has sent you to teach us. Your miraculous signs are evidence that God is with you."

(John 3:1)

The ultimate experience of Africa to me is sunset. I have yet to encounter something more glorious than a sunset cruise down the Zambezi River above the Victoria Falls.

We arrived at the river boat at late afternoon and set sail up the mighty Zambezi. We settled back to enjoy a glass of wine and snacks. The boat quietly chugged up the river alongside the banks and islands as we looked at birds and wildlife. We were rewarded by seeing a variety of birds, as well as hippopotami that bobbed up and down in the water, opening their great yawning mouths. We could hear the evening chirping of the birds as they circled, argued, and settled in the branches of trees for the night. We listened to the call of some animals and were fortunate enough to see a number of warthogs as they dipped to drink at the water's edge. We passed a stately kudu bull with his spiral horns, strolling along the riverbank, also come to get his evening drink.

After a pleasant couple of hours cruising up the Zambezi River we watched the sun start to slowly sink down the horizon. The water gently lapped against the sides of the boat. The green landscape morphed into deep purple shadows. Palm trees stood out as silhouettes against the glowing sky. The path of the sun across the water turned the river into molten gold. I have only ever seen such an exquisite sunset on the Zambezi. We sat in awe appreciating every glowing color of God's palette, a glorious ending to the day. Near the equator, the sun sinks quite quickly, and it was soon below the horizon and it was time to head back to the hotel. We left the boat with a sense of having met with God in the peace and awe of His Creation.

In the Jewish culture, sunset signifies the end of the day. The outcasts, sick, and demon-possessed came to Jesus secretly after dark to be healed. These people were afraid of what others may say or think. A Jewish leader in law and religion, Nicodemus, came to Jesus after dark when he wanted to find out more and have his questions answered.

Sunset is the time of day when we are told to put our worries aside and any anger and problems behind us. If we have experienced a difficult day and hold grudges or anger against someone, Scripture warns us not to let the sun set on our anger. If we have questions to ask, we can lay them down now. There is a good reason for this emotionally and spiritually. When we bring all the troubles of the day to God and ask for forgiveness from those whom we have upset during the day or who have upset us, our minds are stilled. Our hearts can be ready and open to receive answers and love from God again as we worship Him. A clear conscience and mind will let us have untroubled sleep. In the morning, we will be in the right frame of mind to let love flow back into our lives and find solutions to our problems.

The setting sun on the Zambezi was a glowing reminder to me that I should always honor God.

•Are you looking for answers to questions that you are afraid to ask publicly?

•Is there anyone you need to forgive?

•What would it feel like to close your day with a clear conscience and an open heart?

Father, I lay down the burdens of this day at your feet, let me forgive those who have hurt me, bless my family and friends, let your love enfold us all that we may be at peace for the night.

8

Preparing a New Home

There is more than enough room in my Father's home. If this were
not so, would I have told you that I am going to prepare a place for you?"
(John 14:2)

"Even the sparrow finds a home, and the swallow builds her nest
and raises her young at a place near your altar, O Lord of Heaven's
Armies, my King and my God!"
(Psalm 84:3)

We sat on the verandah of the Kingdom Hotel at the Victoria Falls, it
was a hot day, and as we enjoyed a cup of tea, we relaxed and looked out
over the water and the trees at the far end of the hotel gardens. The noise
of chattering birds in some large thorn trees overhanging the water caught
our attention. There must have been a hundred or so nests hanging from
the tips of the branches. I had never seen such a big colony in one tree
before. We sat and watched the little males busily working away, chatting
to each other building their nests. These small yellow Southern African
Weaver birds with their black-masked faces were busy threading strips of
reeds and leaves in and out of the little upside-down oval nests. They flew

in and out with strips of greenery hanging from their beaks, then dangled upside down as they clung to the half-constructed habitation as they pushed and pulled the material to form the nest.

The male weaver bird builds the nest, and the female will come to inspect, and if it is not to her liking, she will start to pull it apart, and he will have to begin again. He may have to rebuild the nest several times. These nests have an opening on the underside with a lip to stop the eggs and babies from rolling out. The entrance placement makes it very hard for predators to access the nest, besides building it out over the water. It may take the male between one and two days to complete a nest. We felt quite sorry for the little males when their mate started to pull it to pieces, and he would have to start from scratch!

Once the nest is complete, the male will defend his territory around his nest and display it to the female to get her approval to move in. Once she is happy with the nest, he adds a short entrance tunnel, and she will move in and make it home by lining the interior with feathers, down, and soft grass heads. Once she has settled in, she will lay up to five eggs, which she sits on for about 12 days until they hatch. The male will help her in feeding the chicks until they can fly in about three weeks.

As I watched the birds building their homes, it reminded me of when Jesus told his disciples that he was going to prepare a place for them, as in His Father's house, there were many mansions. Jesus also said to one of the religious leaders that the birds have their nests, but the Son of Man has no place to lay His head; he said this to indicate the cost of following Him. Yet to the disciples, He said, He was going to prepare a home for them. We all need a home, a roof over our heads, a place to feel safe and secure. Sometimes life puts us in a place where we do not have a dwelling we can call our own; we may have had to give up a home to follow a calling or serve others. Part of the cost of following Christ can be giving up your home.

I have moved home several times locally, but four times internationally; it was always stressful to find a new place to live and reorient myself to my new surroundings. I have never been without some roof over my head at any time, but I have been a total stranger in some of the places I lived, having to start from scratch to make new friends and connections. When I retired and moved internationally again to be near my family, I could not have my own home for various reasons, but my son welcomed me into his home. Retirement was a hard adjustment after a lifetime of being independent to live in a family household again.

Another passage in the Psalms says that the sparrows and swallows build nests and find a home near the Lord God's altar. It is a beautiful thought, the protection and provision of the Almighty not only for the birds of the air for which He provides freely, but for us too as we live close to His heart. When we worship, praise, and pray at the Throne of God, He provides our shelter and sustenance. We do not have to be concerned about being homeless, as Jesus tells us our heavenly Father knows our needs, and He will provide our daily requirements if we make the Kingdom of God our primary concern.

The weaver birds' colony reminded me that God promises us a place in one of many mansions; we will not be living independently. It will not be one person, one mansion; we will be living with whom God has placed us in that home, in one of the many rooms. Are we going to be territorial, like the weaver bird defending his nests, or are we going to live harmoniously with our neighbors? Will we be with our earthly families or our church families?

As I pondered these questions, it made me realize that we need to get along with everyone we know here on earth. The Kingdom of Heaven is within us, so when we get to our room in our allocated mansion, we will be able to live harmoniously with our mansion companions. Are we busy preparing our hearts with the Kingdom of Heaven, loving, and accepting our companions here on earth, ready for our room in the mansion? Or are we being like the little female weaver, tearing our homes apart as we are not entirely satisfied with them? Fortunately, the small weaver bird male has the patience to rebuild the nest until his mate is happy. God also had patience with us, gently growing the Kingdom of Heaven within us until we are gracious and accepting of His provision and protection.

- What is your concept of the home in heaven that Jesus has gone to prepare?

- What evidence have you had in your life that God provides for you?

- How does this help you prepare for the room in the 'mansion' Jesus has gone to prepare?

- Is there anything you are not happy with that God needs patience with you?

"Dear Heavenly Father, thank you for provision for my daily needs. I confess I am not always happy with the things you provide for me. Help me to grow in love for you and acceptance of your provision and protection. Help me to always grow in love toward my 'mansion' companions here on earth so we can live harmoniously both here and, in the mansion, you have prepared for us."

9

My Faith Journey From Legalism To Liberation

This story is my faith journey from a fundamental church background to finding God in Contemplative prayer and meditation freeing my spirit to find God's love.

I was born to parents who belonged to a restrictive fundamental church; they were strict and fanatically religious and believed in spare the rod and spoil the child. I grew up believing that God was an angry, vengeful God who was ready to cast me into Hell if I did not believe and that I could never please him. At a young age, I gave my life to Christ out of sheer terror of being thrown into Hell. As a child, you experience God through your parents, and as I could never please them, my belief of never being good enough stuck. The only love I experienced at that time was through my grandparents and aunts.

I left school and went to live and work in the town, where I attended another legalistic church. Soon I met a young man. We were married young; neither of us had experienced what true love encompassed. After nineteen years of marriage, we divorced, leaving me to raise the children.

There was no help to be found at the churches with legalistic teachings on marriage and divorce.

The divorce was the turning point in my life. I was broken, not only mentally, emotionally, spiritually, but physically as well. I had a neck injury; I did not know if I could work again. I was in an awful place as a single parent. One morning a passage in Psalm 34 caught my attention about God's provision and protection. That was a pivotal moment in my life. Did I believe this vengeful God could take care of me? That passage challenged me. Did I trust what I read? The Church teaching had broken my Spirit. Up to that time, the Bible was just words, written in the King James Version; I had been 'saved' and baptized because that was all I knew to be accepted. I decided to believe in my heart and not my head what the Psalmist said. That was when the miracles started to happen. The Lord began to provide for me even before He began to speak to me.

I found an excellent job that enabled me to buy an apartment. I started to hunger and thirst to get to know this God. I found myself in a phenomenal Methodist church whose focus was on preaching and practical love. I experienced a considerable amount of healing through the teaching on the Holy Spirit and though small groups. Getting to know the God of Love who loved me despite the divorce was a completely new journey for me. I grew spiritually and mentally; in time, I became a small group leader in the Singles Ministry and ran Divorce Recovery workshops.

I had to unlearn so much of the Bible's fundamentalist interpretation, and it is still part of my journey, overwriting legalistic thinking with

33

grace. I had visions and dreams as a teenager of being an artist and writer. I could not pursue them, as I believed I must sacrifice my desires. I now understand God gives you the dreams and desires because that is how he has designed you to provide for you and be a blessing to others.

I grew and matured in my faith, but I still had more to learn. The next part of my journey in getting to know this God of love and grace was when I married again. My second husband was a good and kind man, and we had a loving relationship. I needed to experience what true love felt like and be able to set some boundaries I had not previously been allowed to do. My husband was a diabetic, and after 15 years, he became ill with vascular dementia, which was challenging to manage. The church we attend was also fundamentally inclined. They did not understand dementia and objected to his challenging behavior. My husband decided to go back to the Dutch Reformed church in which he grew up. So, I went with him. I had to function in a second language. I found incredible love and compassion there. I learned about using your spiritual gifts to become more effective. My concept of God changed again. He had given me these gifts, hidden in my desires when I was a child who wanted to paint and write. That was the means he gave me to provide for me and to serve others. All these pieces of the jigsaw puzzle of this God, who loves me, were starting to come together. I learned to be open to God to allow him to provide through whatever means He will. I experienced the tangible love of God through this community as they supported me through my husband's passing. I found that God works globally in different languages and ways and reading the Word in other languages helped make it more understandable.

There were more lessons to learn. After my husband died, I went to the UK to be near one of my children. God miraculously provided a job managing a Christian Retirement home. I had to serve those holding the old legalistic beliefs I had now replaced. I had to show compassion and love to these people; I had to learn to love my 'enemies.' I knew that God was working in and through me to soften hearts and test my faith in His provision and love.

I had time to persevere with the gifts and talents that the Lord gave me. I completed a writing course and joined the local Arts community. God provided opportunities for me to have articles and photographs published, confirming His plan. I learned that God's path is an exciting adventure, day by day, not knowing what each day will bring but trusting anyway.

A family crisis knocked me off-center for a while with news that I felt I could not share for fear of judgment from my legalistic residents. This crisis threw me back on God again, asking Him to teach me what this all meant. Once again, He showed me that love and compassion are the only way through. Sometimes, He has to break your heart so it can expand and grow to love even more. My black and white mindset had to change into rainbow-colored thinking.

My spiritual journey continues, God leading me deeper and deeper into His mystery. Sometimes He is tangible in his love and provision, and sometimes I need to trust. I have found that sitting with God in nature and the stillness of solitude is where I feel His presence most. The way of contemplative prayer and art is also how He designed me to hear His voice and share it with others.

Knowing God is a journey; He puts circumstances, people, and events in your life so that you can experience Him tangibly through them, or He uses you as a channel for others to experience Him. I live with an expectancy that He is speaking to me in whatever I am doing at this moment. I'm learning to live knowing that God loves and cares for me and has planned my path, even though I don't always understand it. I've experienced human love; I needed to know what love is to change my concept of God. God sent Jesus in human form so people could experience God in the flesh, we all need someone that we can relate to, and Christ is that person who became like us. We also need to be Christ to others so they can relate to God through us.

My spiritual life is a journey of being transformed by the renewing of my mind. God is not outside of me; the Kingdom of God is within me. He is in and around me in His creation, peoples, and languages. You can learn about Him from the Bible but need to experience Him within, as well as through his Word.

If you have not yet begun to know God, ask Him to find you and reveal Himself to you, then open your heart to embrace Him as that Spirit who loves you, cares for you, and sent His Son Jesus to show the way.

My Father God, I will trust you, though I walk in dark places you will be with me and I will not have to walk alone. Sometimes I doubt you exist and yet deep in my being I know you are there. Reveal yourself to me Lord in a way I can understand. Amen

About the Author

Deryn is a writer, artist, and lover of nature and travel. Born in the previously named Rhodesia (now Zimbabwe) from 1820 Settler pioneering stock, she has travelled the world, moving to South Africa and the United Kingdom. She retired from her career of an exploration cartographer and housing manager and now lives in the United States of America. Her rich adventures have enabled her to write about transforming life's experiences.

Deryn is a contributing author/illustrator to several books and has had travel articles published in the Senior Travel Expert and contributed to PFS in-house magazine. She writes for her blog "Crossing My Bridges" which is about transitions through grief, new destinations, and the second half of life. She has also contributed to "How 7 Women of Faith Manifest GODLY Success Through Spiritual Intimacy," an Amazon Bestseller in the Christian Liberation Section.

NOTE FROM THE AUTHOR: *If you enjoyed these meditative reflections on African Landscapes and would like to read my blog and get a Newsletter from time to time, please sign up for my mailing list on "Crossing My Bridges".*

Made in the USA
Las Vegas, NV
28 February 2021

18723132R00026